Meet the Horses

Miniature Horses

by Rachel Grack

Bullfrog Books

Bullfrog Books, an imprint of Jump! Library by FlutterBee

Ideas for Parents and Teachers

Bullfrog Books let children practice reading informational text at the earliest reading levels. Repetition, familiar words, and photo labels support early readers.

Before Reading

- Discuss the cover photo. What does it tell them?
- Look at the picture glossary together. Read and discuss the words.

During Reading

- "Walk" through the book with the reader. Discuss new or unfamiliar words. Sound them out together.
- Look at the photos together. Point out the photo labels.

After Reading

- Prompt the child to think more. Ask: Have you ever seen a miniature horse? How small was it?

Bullfrog Books are published by Jump!
3500 American Blvd W, Suite 150
Bloomington, MN 55431
www.jumplibrary.com

Jump! is a division of FlutterBee Education Group.

Library of Congress Cataloging-in-Publication Data

Names: Koestler-Grack, Rachel A., 1973– author
Title: Miniature horses / by Rachel Grack.
Description: Bloomington, MN: Jump!, Inc., [2026]
Series: Meet the horses | Includes index.
Audience: Ages 5–8
Identifiers: LCCN 2025013701 (print)
LCCN 2025013702 (ebook)
ISBN 9798896622383 (hardcover)
ISBN 9798896622390 (paperback)
ISBN 9798896622406 (ebook)
Subjects: LCSH: Miniature horses—Juvenile literature
Classification: LCC SF293.M56 K64 2026 (print)
LCC SF293.M56 (ebook)
DDC 636.1/09—dc23/eng/20250624
LC record available at https://lccn.loc.gov/2025013701
LC ebook record available at https://lccn.loc.gov/2025013702

Editor: Katie Chanez
Designer: Molly Ballanger
Content Consultant: Becky Robb Hotzler; Wells Creek Wild Mustang Sanctuary; This Old Horse, Inc.

Photo Credits: Eric Isselee/Shutterstock, cover; GlobalP/iStock, 1; cynoclub/Adobe Stock, 3, 22; Dotana/Adobe Stock, 4; Juniors Bildarchiv GmbH/Alamy, 5, 23tr; OlesyaNickolaeva/Shutterstock, 6–7; Abramova_Kseniya/iStock, 8, 23tl, 23bl; Vera Zinkova/Shutterstock, 9, 23tm; Sarah/Adobe Stock, 10–11; Norman Eggert/Alamy, 12–13, 23bm, 23br; William Thomas Cain/Getty, 14–15; James Kirkikis/Dreamstime, 16–17; Maskot/Getty, 18; Kids Home Modeling/iStock, 19; Cavan Images Micro/Cavan Images/SuperStock, 20–21; Mark J. Barrett/Adobe Stock, 24.

Printed in the United States of America at Corporate Graphics in North Mankato, Minnesota.

Table of Contents

Small Horses

Small horses play.

They are **miniature**!
miniature horse

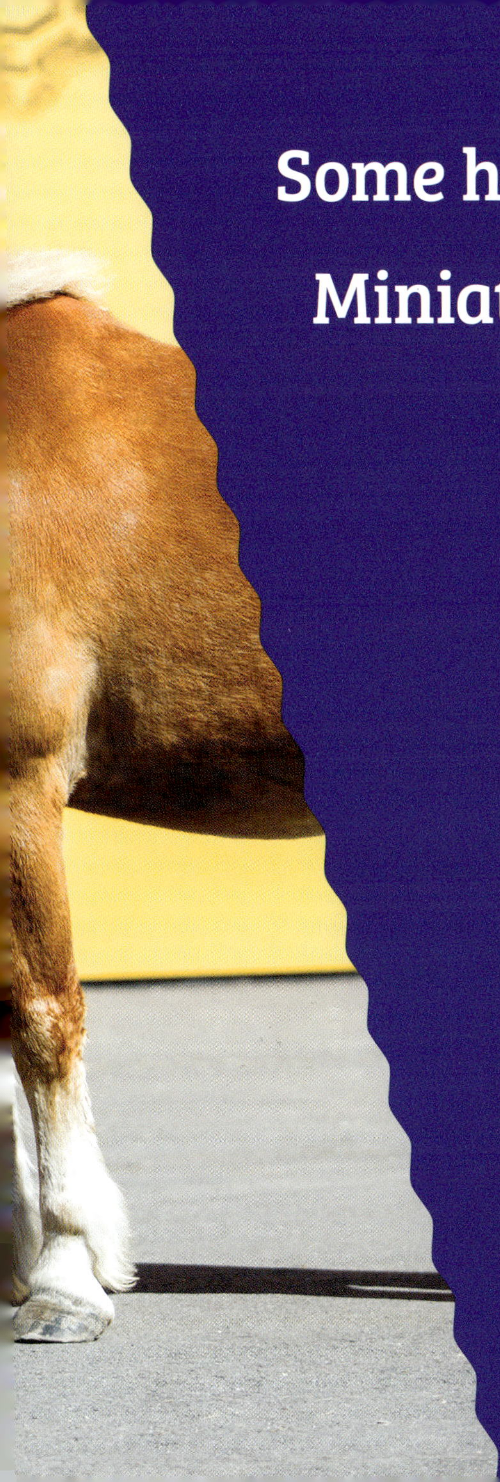

Some horses grow big.

Miniature horses stay small.

Bear's **coat** has a white mark.
She is a **pinto**.

Dusty's **mane** is white.

Buzz has big eyes.

They are far apart.

Rex is smart.

His **trainer** leads him.

He learns **tricks**.

He jumps!

Penny helps people.

Good girl!

DO NOT TOUCH
Service Animal on Duty

Lola pulls us in a sled.

Fun!

Mom feeds Peanut.
I brush his coat.

I walk Oreo.

Small horses love big hugs!

They are good pets.

A Look at a Miniature Horse

What are the parts of a miniature horse? Take a look!

Picture Glossary

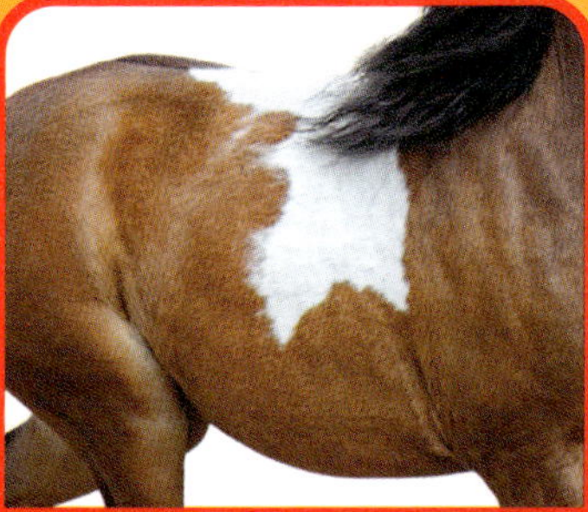

coat
The hair on a horse.

mane
The long hair on a horse's head and neck.

miniature
Something small for its kind.

pinto
A horse with white and dark patches on its coat.

trainer
Someone who teaches horses.

tricks
Special skills that are fun to watch.

Index

To Learn More

Finding more information is as easy as 1, 2, 3.

1. Go to **www.factsurfer.com**
2. Enter "**miniature horses**" into the search box.
3. Choose your book to see a list of websites.